T0150669

An Equal Light

AN EQUAL LIGHT
CHRISTOPHER
JACKSON

THE **BLACK SPRING**
PRESS GROUP

First published in 2022
Eyewear Publishing, an imprint of The Black Spring Press Group
Grantully Road, Maida Vale, London w9
United Kingdom

Typesetting User Design, Illustration and Typesetting, UK

ISBN-13 978-1-915406-27-9

CONTENTS

For my family Jade, Beau and Allegra

THE LION

Long as I can remember I've been pursued
by a suspicion of yellow at my back:
sometimes I turn, guessing at golden prowl —
or stand cunningly before window reflections,
like a private detective, expert at being followed,
to assess the shape of what sneaks up on me.
Often, I only know its nearness after it's gone:
lost in the ingenuity of love,
or listening only to the bells of some crisis,
I'll not even notice how absolutely
it was licking at my ear, or pawing my hair.
I am aware of its restrained strength,
indistinguishable from encouragement.
It is a good lion this, and sometimes so considerate
and silent with its pads, it can be resting
on my heart for hours, and I do not know it.
I am engaged to a kind of bright violence:
it gnaws at my bones, or tarries claws along neurons.
I am appalled at its nimbleness, how I spin round
knowing it's there, and find myself looking only
at the light as it descends through mountain pine,
the optimistic advertisements on the newsagents;
or the inquisitive look of a patient friend.
Its moods shadow mine: if I'm harsh, it's tolerant;
if indulgent, fierce; if ever I incline
towards impatience, it slows its stride to a lope;
but if I dawdle, then it lets me know
with a roar in the ear, how fast it can move:
it is always rushing into the gaps of me.

DANDELIONS

I know why my son picks
the dandelion seeds
and puts them in my pockets
as stowed treasure:
he wants the world to last forever,
and needs
to feel life can be held in store.

I know, because I do
the same:
and photograph
with my enduring mind
each dandelion he finds:
I also aim
to outlive the wind.

THE WATCH

Given to me in the geological past,
it was the promise of my grandfather
never to leave my side, not to die.
I wore it everywhere: in the shower
and in the night, until steam's cunning —
or else some scandal time visits
on whatever seeks to regulate it —
went into the cogs, and the machinery
and spoiled its intricacy, stopping it dead.

Having smiled at humanity for ninety years
my grandfather died... was it the year after?

This morning I looked at it — still in my
possession, a treasure I've not lost.
It tells no time. It is dumb about the day.
But then, I think, isn't that truer?
Sequence isn't really what we have,
if we have memory to circumvent it.
Last and first feel joined up — and death
has something to do, after all, with breath,
or breathing. With water and air.
My grandfather said death let the sun in —
and he always said it with a grin,
knowing it a thought to make me brave.

Having smiled at humanity for ninety years,
my grandfather found final recompense
out of the amphitheatre of human tears,
and into the divine audience.

HONEYEATER

The honeyeater has forgotten all its song.
It sits alone in the Hundred Acre Wood:
its tongue is knotted, and its day feels wrong.

Not to meet kindred is to forget singing —
in our sad hour, that much is understood:
the honeyeater has forgotten all its song.

There was once a time of unending spring.
I yearn for that more musical world
when tongues weren't knotted, days never wrong.

Now at noon, the signature shadows throng,
in a way which doesn't — cannot — be good:
the honeyeater has forgotten its song.

Such beauty here used to ring along
the birch and willow, as if we kept a stronghold:
that was before knots in bird-tongues, days so wrong.

Will we sing again? At its core life's strong,
and throats untie. Things come right — or should.
But the honeyeater has forgotten its song.
Its tongue is knotted. The day feels wrong.

DYLAN

On hearing 'Murder Most Foul'

I hope that when the world grows silent,
parties disband, and dancing feet suspend
there will always be one to wheel the piano out
and dare the world to start again.

I hope there'll always be the voice of the seer
telling that song is the other side of murder,
that there's kingliness in melody,
and that power lies in your creative day.

I hope there'll always be some wise wraith
who makes the young pause when they hear him —
and lets them know that all the ancient faiths
are likelier true than any fad or whim.

I hope — and find the answer in this song.
I think it threads backwards out of here
and away and down to something so strange and strong
no conspirator can make it disappear.

WOOD-VOICE

after 'The Dream of the Rood'

It was years ago. I was felled —
upended, bundled along the clearing,
up a mossy ridge and along a verge
where an incision of light, like a nail,
was laughed at by ducks marooned in a pond:
I expected to be a gallows for bandits.
I was shouldered to a hilltop,
and wedged into the earth's pliancy.
He came to me almost quickly,
and fastened himself to my stoicism:
I accepted a human weight;
the nails were painful for me also.
I looked down on my brothers,
the valleyed, emerald or mallow
with superfluity of leaf —
kindred neither sliced and scandalised
and raised up to my eminence,
nor carpentered to my shape of suffering:
I pitied their exclusion.
All the while he rode the jeers underneath,
announcing another knowledge than science:
he said in his still-deep voice
that he was ruled by a jurisdiction
distinct from Caesar's vanity,
or Herod's architecture.
I was implicated in the general mockery.
Blood seeped into my rings, like rust, like paint.
After the insane hour had arrived
and the mother was weeping,

and the disciples panicked,
wondering if they'd still know how to heal,
they undid the bones,
and let the shroud billow.
Rain fell, dampening everything.
I emitted the sodden complaint
of rained-upon wood.

EZEKIEL

Before I knew what I was implicated in,
I had already assented:

the winds suddenly made the clouds busy,
tossing them about the sky,
as if impatient for consummation:
they'd turn them to something else.
As those high fogs sped up,
they accelerated into a metamorphosis,
their interior now was fire —
a light that burned and had some eloquence to convey.

Five birds rushed out of that vision.
Their squawks became vatic fragments of human language.

Something about *a garden*
where all the trees dance, and the urgency to pray
for the broken-hearted now
and at the hour of our death.

And the sky was filled with:
speaking faces
beaks which became mouths
extolling prophecy
flaming mouths
whose tongues licked fire.

Do not worry. The marvellous is the case.
Let not your heart be troubled. You shall see his face.

Now the voices were bodies,
and the bodies were dancing in a ring:
sweet movement of the angels had swung
out of that light and into the skies.

With a suddenness swifter than thunder,
all that dancing was a voice:

'*Stand up straight! Up straight!*'

The bread-roll was warmly baked next to me
on the stand.
It was strangely sweet to the taste.
Honey pooled infinitely into my hand.

AFTER AESCHYLUS: THE FIRM

There are ludicrous devils in each of these rooms,
perched without your seeing them:
giggling, silly on the reception-desk;
or jabbering in prestigious corner-offices,
they hop along the expensive-suited shoulders
of hot-shot partners; or darken the brow of
ambitious associates: see them laugh and jump,
and flit down stairs, like schoolchildren
breaking up after exams. Or else they point —
without your even knowing that they're there! —
in hilarity at duped clients in lift-mirrors.
They run like rats in the pipes: they *are* the bones
of the architecture — bacterial in glass,
or like a virus infecting its supports.
They fly like spores, an aspect of the air.
They raise pound signs in the eyes of inhabitants,
who have an obscure penalty to pay:
none who comes here is ever truly happy.
But when Dike, daughter of Themis, descends
on this house, on a certain auspicious day,
then the spider-spirits and the half-dead bat-ghouls
shall leave, and the sun shaft in, showing
not dust-motes as in an attic skylight,
but all the dying devils, galled by her power,
and a new dominion shall be founded,
and the force of the demons be re-channelled
towards the better health of the polity.

A CERTAIN MORNING

Never before had I longed for any tombside.
The dew and the spices, potioned together,
gave the air its fresh pelt, and look of lion hide.
Somewhere in the depth of nature: laughter.

Suddenly, unexpectedly, we were running,
rediscovering speed. Need was nearly over,
the ancient hope to know the reason for things.
All the hills were turned to four-leafed clover.

Plover flitted above our pace, a pair dipped —
then flew down the levels, as if to celebrate.
Prostrate on the tomb — muzzled, black-lipped —
was the animal we were here to assimilate.

The sun on the grass became a mane;
the wind become a roar encompassing time.
Wherever I walk, I hear its enormity again,
saying with power, *redeem, redeem, redeem.*

THE LUKE SONNETS

I.

Rigor and vigour
are all I have
with which to describe the strange:
it is better than a pitch for credulity,
Theophilus.

I have been through documents,
comparing each with each,
verified conjecture against fact,
held it all up to candlelight:
I've squinted with scrutiny,
sceptical as an atheist,
to figure out
what was left:
the magic paper that doesn't burn.

II.

I am certain of Herod:
his reign is written in all the annals
and is not contested:
and it's known that in Judaea
at that time
there was Zechariah, a priest,
of Abijah's division.
His wife, Elizabeth,
was one of Aaron's daughters.

God knew them each to be truthful —
inclined towards kindness,
and without any
weave of scheme about their hearts:
devout folk.

III.

They'd never heard
the sharp wail babies make
as they leave the womb,
and arrive reddened in the world.
And would not — time
was at their hips and knees,
universally in the flesh.

Though badged with disappointment,
they were bound in love,
and a wholly
appropriate hope:

it's natural to consider the sky,
take note of this world-theatre,
and hope a little.

IV.

Zechariah would perform his offices:
he did so alone,
treading altar-wards while outside

the multitudes prayed,
offering up need of healing,
or richer dialogues
with God: communion-thought,

when God and man,
by the bestowed
skill of consciousness
inhabit their need of each other.

Zechariah would burn incense:
and watch the scents of smoke
rising into rafters.

V.

They never heard afterwards
precisely what was said:
they only saw the man rendered dumb,
and noticed instead
the naked and speech-deprived face
mobile with wonder.

He was new:
cloaked in a suspicion of light,
light also at the eye-points.

Some said he had been singled out
for some mission.
No one doubted that some gigantic good
must come out of whatever encounter
he had had beside the altar.

VI.

Years later, we heard it from him direct:
how the outsized angel,
like a giant, wings heaven-knitted like feathery rainbows,
had presented itself,
a being outside his experience:

an otherness
addressing the priest's amazement
with solid predictions.

Elizabeth is altered:
Her womb shall entail a child,
One who shall make the people raucous for God.

There shall be nothing trivial about him.
He shall meet the world
Injected with higher purposes.

PAST, PRESENT, FUTURE

I met Past on the corner of Gloucester Road and Cromwell Road, examining the moon as if about to confide in it. Its skull was strong, its skin papyrus-ish. It looked on Present with exasperation as it tied obsequious garlands around its ankles. I knelt next to Present and looked up from shadows of bulk. I turned to meet its eye: its features were white, its eyes florid like one of those blue-eyed freckled types who throughout life seem always about to enter convulsions. It whispered that someone round the corner was intent on its immediate murder. Embarrassed, I stood up and spoke again with Past, ignoring Present altogether. As I was quizzing it about its attire, tittering about its scars and medallions, the dignity of its height quaked. Future walked towards us, seven times our height, kicking at bins, singing its anthem. Something about how it would never suffer itself to fail.

MEET MR ROCKWELL

And this is Mr Rockwell, fixture of the bank,
straight and white as a Greek pillar, eh, Rockwell?
Newspapers invent villainy to hide their own.
Harmless, this fellow. But a passion for pensions, eh, eh?
That's Rockwell smiling. A forgettable face, no doubt,
without distinguishing feature — ideal for crime! —
a little pockmarked perhaps, ghost-farms of acne,
the head not yet egg-bald but you're losing it
I suspect Mr Rockwell. He never answers.
What else? Non-descript teeth, a collar-like neck,
you can't really tell the nape of him from the shirt,
yet an unarguable face, it couldn't be otherwise.
Of course, it's not the best face, not a Hollywood face.
You can't always people the world with heroes.

DEVILS

Above is hurtle, the horror of blizzard.
Cloud and ice disparage the distant
fire of the moon, and the world is snow:
Heaven and night are lost to us.
The coach advances, the bells insist
on themselves with tintinnabulations...
We drift along the vast unknowable.
Inside, we have become our terror.
Step on it, cabbie! 'Sorry sir, can't sir:
It's the horses, sir: good as dead, sir.'
I am turned to whir, almost blinded
by the mastery of snow, its flight and tussle.
'Sir, I'm just going to be straight:
we left the trail several hours ago.
But then that was the devil, you see?
What can you do when he whirls at you?
There! See him? Jolly and at play,
like a bellows puffing in front of us.
You missed him — there! — in the spinney —
and there! — making the horse hysterical.
Look, this time: right in front of us,
that strange smiling trickster,
close, closer, and now so large,
practically afire, and now lost to the dark.'
Above is hurtle, the horror of blizzard,
cloud and ice disparage the distant
fire of the moon, and the world is snow:
Heaven and night are lost to us.
It's unsustainable, all this whirling!
You see, even the bell has lost its voice,
the horses are lame... *Hey, cabbie, what's happening?*

'Damned if I know — a stump? A beast...'
The blizzard grows and modulates.
Horses labour with frightened breath;
I see the horrendous shape of his flight.
We strain through the air to see him,
the horses arrest and rear, and the bell
is a dutiful catastrophe of tinkling...
Finally I see the strange commotion:
these now are the evil spirits,
a gang of grotesques, whirling in allegiance
with the haze of the milky moon:
lilting, fluttering, and all a-swirl
like leaves mid-air in autumn-time...
That's some crowd! Do they have a destination?
What song is that, plaintive, like a lament?
It's as if a demon were being interred,
or a witch had duped a good man into nuptials.
Above is hurtle, the horror of blizzard,
cloud and ice disparages the distant
fire of the moon, and the world is snow:
Heaven and night are lost to us.
The devils have swarmed into our journey,
they are rushing around with utter license.
The valley is now a boundless complaint.
My poor heart is the screech of their mockery.

from the Russian of Alexander Pushkin

POEM FOR VICTORIA DAY

When I see you build your plastic tower
on the eve of Victoria Day
and render it ambitious, until your sister
comes and knocks it all away,
you cry, and stomp and throw
your body on the floor. I know
you have a fair point to make.
Night cedes. Victoria Day comes —
and you are asked to take
'something Victorian' for your class.
But the past has gone under the grass;
it has evaporated into the skies.
If work isn't stored, shall we say it dies?
If I didn't guess at some structure
in and between the fading architecture
which respects — adores — our efforts,
I might join you by your broken forts
and weep a little, and then some more.
But because I do thirst for that justice,
and because I know the earth contains
flowers as well as skeletons
I try optimism on for size,
and tell you that the ultimate prize
is for those who insist on labour.
Saying all that, I plant a kiss
on your tears, and help you off the floor.

THE CONSECRATION

Let this arise then, let a certain scale amass.
Let all the murdered and the exhausted —
those who gasped with knees on their throats,
those who met their deaths in loneliness —

have quadrangles in which to console their pain,
pilasters decorated with Ambitious Mind,
and apses so muscular on the tongue, we'll find
that one day we can say we tasted the rain

in the flesh of thistles. That we wrought a beaker of sun
out of all those times of reprehensible heat.
And stood that glass on the table and raised a beat
which announced ourselves a people who'd done

what we needed in order to grow wise and learn.
And found the fruit by nibbling round the rind.
And learned solace in the bone-riddled ground.
And saw the earth stir. And heard the stone turn.

DAYS

Each day grants us its particular thing:
slug, snug in the watering-can's neck;
robin, on the fence, worm-wondering.
There was the time we took the frozen milk

and placed it trophy-like on the table
and watched the roof cease to block the sun
until the look and strength of marble
was burned away, and unfrozen.

We placed it inside, and poured our prize.
In time, we took the garden in hand:
mended the decimation of the grass,
learned the exact species of sand

the lavender likes, and the patience
which the sunflower possesses
in the kernel. If ours was a sentence,
it was a benign one spent amid roses —

hardly a hardship at all.
It began to seem to us necessary:
Will the giant know himself tall
if he is always solitary?

We did not know our mind's secret music
until we stood in that garden —
staggered to find the range of beauty
whose freedom is to alight on anyone.

EASTER, 2020

The flowers of the earth are not meant to fail:
already this morning, I have guessed at one
who began early, in the parks of Camberwell,
sprinkling crocus along the shafts of the sun.

It once seemed foolish to endorse creation,
and bear witness to the silver on the cheeks of cherries.
Some say there's no sound basis for the human;
and platitudinous good too often miscarries.

But the flowers of the earth are not meant to fail:
out on the slopes, there is evidence
for any who will submit themselves to the spell:
there is more than death in the ambit of the lens.

Today, be grateful that the flowers cannot rid
themselves of beauty: that one was up this day
before sleep was washed off a single eyelid
and sprinkled crocus along our twisting pathways.

UPPER

In these grounded days,
decide to love
the uppermost in things:
cloud in its barge pace;
the summits of trees,
where branch-tips whiten
in a confusion of light;
consider the paths of birds —
the swallow's sudden dips,
the sky-roll of gull,
or the flustered robin,
always learning
something new about air;
enjoy the building-tops,
the silver slopes of roofs,
TV aerials, those
emblems of our cleverness;
chimney-metal-light,
or smoke's incense climb
as if the city were
a ceremony and we all
worshipped at its edge;
praise the seedlings
whipped up high,
or lost helium balloons,
which are a child's heartbreak
hoisted in the sky;
be in awe of
what the imagination might
in a trice produce:
stray spacecraft blast

and fragments of asteroid
burned by something
unfriendly in our
congenial atmosphere;
be in praise of
the claim of lapis lazuli,
the whites of cloud
so confident in themselves
until they are upended
as earth renews
its nightly drift
from the sun, a high fact
told in suites of red
and pinks and yellows.

'I THINK OF THOSE WHO FELL BIZARRELY SILENT'

I think of those who fell bizarrely silent:
Sibelius grand and speechless in Järvenpää,
who descended so quietly toward the grave:
decades-sedentary, in private tinker
with an outline. He would rest considerate
of the truer music which lies always at the gates
of the ear. Neither timid nor brave,
he was suspended in the shape of an endeavour.

I think of those who fell bizarrely silent:
Rimbaud, running guns in Africa,
his letters bare of poetry. He seems,
in each bald missive, an improbable imposter
on the self that could construe *Seasons of Hell*:
and gave himself over to the commercial
as if trying to forget what was hard to redeem:
London and Verlaine, the unbreathable disaster.

I think of those who fell bizarrely silent:
Shakespeare, with gianthood secreted in New Place,
where autograph-hunters never craved to go:
departed neither in glory nor disgrace
quiet about poetry and family feud,
neither validated nor misconstrued —
as if in wintertime he only knew
or cared to think of death's last grace.

I think of all these as our silence lasts
and augments, and changes as it grows:
I think of the power lodged in restraint,

how the high deed is always juxtaposed
with waiting, the huge wonder of a pause.
We need not always have a claim or a cause —
but may stand at death's foothills without complaint
and discharge in peace the burdens of the snow.

DORA'S FIELD

The pike lifted, and levelled in clear zenith.
An immensity, European in scale,
like the alps he'd later grapple with
in *The Prelude*: why should nature not pull

the dead back from their having died
if it can do this — melt and mould rock
into sculpture, and raise up these bulbs
from clods to petal-veins a tongue can lick?

They patted them together, grief-inspired.
They stooped, their seventy years bent to hope,
and found a task there fit for hurt hearts.
To plant was to cope. It was not to stop.

Faith is work. Because work is continuing,
and in that decision is trust: to see
things through beyond the bitter conclusion
into good habits of mind where self-pity

isn't: to construe a thread of light
out of the confusions of the dark wood,
and prove it true against all fear:
courage is the sum of what is withstood.

ELEGY FOR A MAN I NEVER MET

i.m c.j

I invoke the ending-up of Christo James:
more than a name, I will vouch for him
before all tribunals, though I never once
saw the way light caught his eye
or damaged his flesh. How often does
ritual of friend request lead to
gentle salutations on your timeline?
It is enough. In the swift and painful world
it has to be: most people are not encountered,
not even our own selves are really known.
Yet something of him, realer than
death, was, without my knowing it, meteoric
along my life. I honour the blaze of him. And will state
of the poet I've not yet read, and didn't meet,
that if there is no place for him in the gigantic scheme
then this is not quite the universe for us.

SKATE MUSIC

Everything went wintry. You skated out
like a tired traveller — an image of fading skill,
done with the old limits. Each scrape of fate
came smaller, and we watched you skirl
until you were out of reach of sight or ear,
free and final as a well-phrased thought.

I clutched at the verdict of your skates:
their scratches tiny as voles, and your figure
a silhouette almost lost to weight.
I feared the contents of those mountain-trees
before death shuffled behind me in the leaves.

Out of shadow now, the unearthly call:
a demon swooping in sheets of night-breeze,
bent on giving terror its absolute and all,
while I remembered all that you had taught.

For a moment, you were moon-held, toiling away
from red claws which aimed to claim your day —
into the un-life of mountain-shadow.

I heard nothing; saw no sign of you.
I could only hope that if you'd been skating here,

you must have found viable ice out there.

IN MEMORIAM JEREMY HEYWOOD (1961–2018)

Almost unknown; scaling uprights:
the circus' seasoned acrobat
who knew the balancing routines —
the huddled faces low, upturning.

If it was an act, it seemed necessary:
a staged anonymity,
sought and found in life's tumult,
whose skill slipped, a missed vault,

which showed what once had passed for truth:
how he and his sort had smoothed
absurdist shapes of disparate folly;
silent effort mastering belly-cries,

linking the uncodified.
His absence showed the aftermath clear:
lions tore at the elephant hide,
in absence of the circus-master.

Now at show's end, whispers rise,
and all turn as they depart the tent.
Was there dirt under nail? Motes in his eyes?
The auditorium will not fall silent

so long as we performed at all.
There were too many watchers; and each
gets implicated in the other's pall —
fallibility, most of what we have to teach.

MASS

As I walk along the massy world I laugh:
the locusts ate the bread in the cupboard,
and the moths nibbled at my scarf.
The lawyers filched all the biscuits in the jar,
my toys have been dismembered and gored,
but I was too heavy, too heavy by far.

As I go through the daffodil parks, I slow:
the world is now too capable of being hard.
With a hey, and a ho, and a hey nonny no
it wrecked my bank, and exploded my car;
where my house had windows, it now has lakes of shard,
because I was too heavy — too heavy by far.

As I went into the vacant house, I cried:
I was proud, and you gave my back a stoop.
I was confident; that died with my pride.
And then I dreamed along Gennesaret's shores
that the lion tried, and failed to pick me up,
saying, 'You are too heavy, too heavy by far.'

Now as I go along life's walks, I chant:
O, bring me all the people who are desolate;
fetch me those who want to love but can't.
let deprivation be a lightening of our store
and preparation for the departure date.
We are all too heavy, too heavy by far.

DIARY CLASH

for Clive James, on having been unable to attend his book
launch for The River in the Sky *at his home in Cambridge*

It was no disaster, but I didn't make the party.
I'd come to know brightness, and not light.
I knew the poet better than his verse;
politician better than policy.
Handshakes are really a kind of curse:
the original reason for celebrity
is superior to fame's look.
And success can be a dreary sight:
the faces all togetherness-brightened
at the symposium
I was too France-bound to attend
are worth a modicum
of any one section of their best books.

It's fine not to have made that *soirée*.
It's true that in deferential encounters
I've seen more than fame's weird glow:
an eye-gleam in the interviewee —
like the *pertugio* amid the *Inferno*,
the spark that made them noteworthy
and deserving of renown —
and been grateful to know such apertures.
But I very diligently doubt
that there'd have been much more
than misery at that party which I was out
of the country for:
I imagine a congregation of frowns.

It's good — on this one occasion —
not to make that launch: to have been,
say, harangued in Villefranche-sur-Mer
by an indignant attendant
when, parked by the solemn barrier,
I couldn't read the instructions
in that treacherous ticket machine.
Everything that happens teaches meaning:
now I see how the written word certainly
never prospers amid fuss,
and poems don't need the silly
approval which stems from the tremendous
absurdity of a convening.

Anyone who asks, tell them I'm alright
about having missed it: say that my wife
is formidable; my friends kind.
You may add that after the famous car strife
my boy paddled toward the pebbly sand,
and in the celebrating light
briefly showed that he could swim.
But let's be clear, I'm in a little pain —
and ever since, have been somewhat sad
at being so bound up in obligation and space
as not to travel at a whim
to watch you bask in finishing a poem
which is slated to last
when this feeble lament of mine is past.
What I need now is for it not to happen again.

FRANCIS

It was time to build a civilisation:
in shadows of the dungeon,
next to truckle-bed and straw,
he found a light whose intent was clear.
No sooner had he gripped the secret
and mysteriously laughed at it
than he emerged changed —
and to all who knew him, strange.
He sang in vales as the otters lapped.
The green woodpeckers stopped
their tapping — rapt, rapt at a joy
which grew without delay
into the grandeur of the message
executioners cannot assuage:

The sun is brother to the human throat,
and when I sing it laughs: 'Lend your coat
to the poor that they might not be cold
and inform the rich that they'll soon be old'.

In the spring-awaiting fields,
and along the greening folds
the pestilent and the tired
clutched at the new word:
his life seemed fresh and true —
the first hill's wondrous dew.
Now all the poor hearts were full;
and clamour had come to the people.
Soon, all were busy ushering
their own particular spring,
rushing through sunflower and maize

into new-dimensioned days
where simplicity was
both a brightness and a cause:

The sun is brother to the human throat,
and when we sing it laughs: 'Lend your coat
to the poor that they might not be cold
and tell the rich that they'll soon be old'.

FAIRFIELD

The claim is hard but not impossible:
I have passed this exterior sufficiently
to know the smooth truth: this wall
contains someone I ought to meet frequently.

That brought me to this hour. I knock —
and note the light about the porch-roses,
and consider the footsteps inside, as they track
the source of my separate created noises.

The claim is hard but not impossible:
if this lilac-flanked door were to open
I'd become a completely delighted soul —
there'd be welcome, wine, scent of the cyclamen.

Once made, the claim becomes easier:
some good lives here. All I need is
this wisteria fence; this hint of stairs;
this door about to peel back.

BETWEEN JOBS AT IL PALAGIO

At the point between work and leisure,
rote hours retain their claim in the body,
and will not yet be shed:
they live in the bone, as a signature
of what was necessary this past year and more.
Flip-flop-shod,
without anything particular to do,
I keep appointment with the vineyard path,
walking the patterns of the olive shade,
the ancient curves of Tuscany
the best the world has come up with,
my sole calendar the mountain's tracery.
Toil had this missing in its addictions.
Toil took me away from... What exactly?

Now a cockerel screams,
and renders me leftwards-turning,
towards a portion of what I've needed —
and which I so suddenly see,
it is as if I never held a job nor will again:

indiscriminate wildflower, poppy and daisy,
bank-grasses —
and most of all, the wind playing in all that,
incarnate, and whipping the light,
or the light catching it, just ever so slightly,
in the gaps between the flowers,
and the heart quickening its pace
at something it's seen, and knows again,
having not known this in so long —
that there is a kind of bell that hides in nature,

which we're meant to hear, and even obey,
and I move on, a new role triggered within
which shall keep me busy
this side of things being shaped to the temporal.

RECESSIONAL

Clutter and mess of our possessions
has its interruption at our garden-doors.
We open their fold to admit in miniature
the vigorous entirety of the world.
One by one, bees visit the decking,
on investigative patrol. Here spiders
are cunning also, webbing weed and iron table
setting a trap which flies still fall for,
in spite of all the evolving they've done.
Up steps, the grasses lie in cool clumps,
interspersed with clay and stray shingle,
dandelion, foxglove and unnamed weeds.
I know the deep earth contains the intention
of mushroom, since they whitened our little
rectangle last year. They'll no doubt
opt for repetition since repetition
means life for them: I make no judgements.
The magnolia is next, flowering
in valid brevity at each twist of the axis —
we dug it in last spring, and learned then
the stubbornness of this hill, and the secrets
it will yield only to shoulder and pitchfork:
old building materials left by an Edwardian
or wwii veteran; shard of glass;
a section of brick dumped by a callous hand.
The creepered wall curtails our land:
in shadows snails crouch in fear of the birds
which peck on the shed-top and in undergrowth:
blue-tit, sparrow and jay vie and dance,
and fetch food for their improvised nests —
themselves fearful of the pantomime foxes,

which sometimes slope with toothy villainy,
in a parade of reclaiming along the grass,
to squeeze under a hole in the fence.
The cat is atop the wall, and slopes off
at the clatter of the two squirrels which —
mating or fighting, we are unable to tell —
rattle round the fencing, over the extension,
and off towards the sleeping next-door houses.
The high fence cedes to next door's stumpy trees
whose cutting we lamented five years ago,
when we woke in grief at their sudden lack,
to take heart in time at what remained:
the satisfying rose-bush at our path's edge,
and the elderflower above, and the apple-tree,
which bends its weight, and bestows its fruit
each year onto our lawn, where we come
with buckets to enact the ritual of gathering.
The world never ends: it has within it
a passion and an ambition which far exceeds
what we can imagine — but even its extent
is just the beginning of the possible:
I suspect there are universes hidden here.
My pledge is that this day, and every other,
I'll go looking for them, and make my breathing
in my grounds the sound of the voyager;
the discoverer; the happy stumbler-upon.

THE SUNFLOWER

Groped skywards in green levels,
    its poise a regular obtaining
    of each five-inch rung.
    Its history is traversed fear,
    time ridden out and made right.
    Underleaves turning sere
    is an aspect of reaching for a light
    borrowed from sky and gravel.
Death's a scorpion, hated even by itself.
    The flower's thirst was to obtain
    what it could of sun and rain —
    and summon to its spoors the bee-wing.
    The lawn's bevelled shelf
    hosted its network of roots
    in inventive cahoots
    with sun to permit a flowering.
That summer, wind wove the fuzzy stalk.
    We wanted it to build beyond pain
    and live without stain —
    bannering with silk green talk
    the garden where we walk.
    Life's a thick ambition to support.
    We watered one with too hard a hose.
  Squirrels nabbed another, and only this one rose
high enough to be the joy poetry and bee-mouth sought.

PECKHAM APPLES

Suspended in gravity's poise —
little chunks of a Cezanne,
distinct in their fruit-sphere
to whatever transpires in ours —
I'd be an ungrateful man
if I didn't pause at these globes,
and say yes, always, to life.
Impassive at the worm's probe
and cheeking the new sun;
compliant with bird and hosting
the wasp's jazzy tunnels;
they contain a stately rebuke
to anything like waste or rush.
This is nature's silent selfhood,
a sort of laminate ruse
of doing what apples do —
doing so well what they can —
which is its own rejection
of the principle of dejection.
They hang there, I want to believe,
as pluckable proofs
of the perfect shape of love:
light-burnished, colour-varnished,
sending in their patient
acceptance of what gravity
will ultimately say to them,
good news to the tired mind.
No wonder that in found papyrus
this food denoted fall.
Contained in these circles
is the story of temptation —

to gorge on crunchy flesh,
and with face smeared and wild,
go with unsourced guilt inside,
and raise the marred residue:
look at what I picked for you.

TREE SHADOW

Not later, now:
study what the trees possess:
interstitial mystery
and the mastery of shadow.
Consider this sacred,
and in rendering that assessment,
love also those passages,
inveterately grand,
where the shafts hardly land
to green or yellow each leaf,
and fail to show their veins
and young flutter. If this is grief,
then it's held in reins
of calm: these dark centres where
confidence pertains
teach us how each flower
possesses the secret of Easter.
They know the ulterior
processes which are the sweet
basis for our life.
Their love of the world is replete
thanks to a unity stored
between delight and strife:
no matter how shadowy
a tree becomes,
I often seem to see a silver
wire thrilling in them,
which is the utmost desire
to be, and resurrect themselves
in sap time and again,
bypassing the scandal of pain

in favour of a power
known to the bird in its hour
but not to us, who stand
in foothills of a death which isn't
worrying about what isn't.

CAT

Quick, the shadow
of a morning cat
pouring itself down our back wall:
like dark wine into an old bottle,
transforming that patch
of earth into a black radiance
filled with
black radiance.

THE SPIDER

On hearing Dusapin's String Quartet No. 6 ('Hapax')

I am, of course, a spider:
my obstinacy, a viola;
my gossamer back-and-forthing,
woven ruminations
of a violin. Watch me,
busy always to continue
a spider's life. All things
love the little kingdom
they inherit. This is home,
intricate with fetched
fidget, this scratchy bow-flight
is a busy cello urging
me to tracery,
all tossed about in
winds of orchestra.
And did you hear that bar
when everything united,
when an abseil's pause
swung, magnified
by a coalescence in the score?
It was as if the sun
saw our swaying,
and hurried to republish
the mystery
of me.

LULLABY

Let him sleep on a little more,
so we might pause and twine fingers
as we did before,
and stay with the memory that lingers
this side of the bedroom door.

Sunlight split the patio
until rains clattered on the hedges.
To watch them with you
was to know the confident perspectives,
and sense with forward view:

that I'd ask you to let him sleep
just a little more, on a day like this,
that we might stare deep
into the luck of our togetherness,
and stow this afternoon in our keep.

THE COAT

You made of your day a coat
intended to keep me warm.
Its sleeves were the hours of one and two;
its collar was the dawn.

You rendered your day a cloak of silk
I would cheerfully put on;
the mid-morning hour a lining
airy and pleasant to don.

You made your afternoon a hood
coloured like the tamarind;
and evening-time a green lapel
to thumb against the wind.

Your night was a loom, contriving
these pockets, these seams.
Its last touches were bestowed
by bright patterned dreams.

Friend, here: take your coat.
Time is awake in it.
It only took a day to make.
And see — it fits.

PANDEMIC TRAIN

It held us there in our fascination:
a train was shunting up
the track, headed for Denmark Hill station.
We waved. The driver gave a parp.

And set the trees shaking like a time machine.
I felt myself roll back
to Russia, and another crisis: the revolution,
as told by Pasternak.

I felt heat: the historic nature of all this —
how a people would be divided,
and return together talking about changes.
The past would be derided

as a thing too innocent, which didn't know about
what we'd be slated to go through.
Now and then, history rucks, we all lose out —
but win also: we go

down life's slope knowing we had some taste
of the seismic, the strange.
And if we rose to that, rose above waste,
and found our range.

THE WIND

Belts us, encircles us — is a part
of us a brief while.
It wants us to rise to the occasion.
Instead we flail.

And if the wind had eyes,
a mouth, a human face?
What would our ribbons of the skies
tell us about grace?

I'd say the outdoors has a kind of
tidying impulse
to rid the reaching mind of
whatever's false:

it's the secret life in verbs;
coaxes, vests, and sways;
augments, recedes, curbs;
whips; plays.

It's our nurse against lament and hurt;
our sealer-up of pain.
It wants to disabuse the heart
of vendettas. Again

it comes round the corners of trees,
tells us that more is possible —
that some surreptitious ease
lies at the gates of the will.

It's our agent, even our minister.
It wants to take my hand, but can't.
It's such a sweet, subtle helper.
And love is its chant.

DIRGE

It was an appointment she had to keep
and she kept it by a sleep.
A thousand lives was not enough
to exhaust the obligations of love.
I miss her. That's my pain.
She'll not be here again.
She'll not be here to see the tree
capitulate to the sea —
for she has gone in her turn
beyond the sea's churn
and the jurisdiction of stars:
outside the universe.
It was an appointment she had to keep
and she kept it by a sleep.
I am exhausted to think of my pain:
she'll not kiss my eyes again.
The universe could not be true
to the love her flesh outgrew:
her life needed to be let out
of the flesh's weary doubt
into her unhindered raiment.
All her life, love was her appointment.

SEAGULL CAUGHT IN SHOP-WINDOW

Around that time, we took note of the birds:
the newly-colourful pigeon; the dominant wren;
the delighted sparrow; the fear-free robin.
They stood beyond our realm of image and word,
urging that we bear witness in the new silence:
to gulls on confident jaunts from Brighton,
and jays roosting in St Giles, their confidence
a pattern which recurred in the greenfinches of Richmond.
Everywhere we turned, there was taking heart
at what ailed humankind, a pestilence
so vigorous it upended the motions of human art,
and sledgehammered the furniture of our mind.

One morning, a blue tit swooped past my shoulder
as we scooted down Camberwell Grove:
along the hawthorn it went, low and brave,
as if it had just been released from some endeavour
it had been loathing. The yard daffodils
looked as though they'd never more deserved
the shadows that it made along their petals:
their pickable glory shone, as my son swerved
down the inveterate old Roman route,
and took the contours of these ancient hills
as a due given to him beyond doubt:
in his balance, springtime was assured.

When another wren departed from an elm,
its rotating flight was my own returning
to that other bird on High Street Kensington,
still further before, in my unmarried time.
It was the seagull, trapped in the storefront

of the clothes store. I held it in mind
as our feet continued, onwards to confront
the windows which the young John Ruskin turned
to French medieval, bringing Chartres
across the channel, to preside over the font
where this same boy would meet the water,
and make that church, for us, sacred ground.

I heard the wing flapping before I saw it:
and took a moment to wonder at its panic:
its sinewy pandemonium, and barking beak
protesting at this realm of folded shirts,
and testing again the solidity of glass
always to his detriment, until frustration
became an inarticulate chaos
of wild hopping, and dire attempts to fly on
through that bogus zone of transparency
into the air it knew: the air beyond our gazes
and the frightened manager, whose misery
had to do with the weight of human dominion.

In time, the gull was poked and persuaded out
of the special hell it had blundered into,
and waddled out into open carpet, the window
an ordeal it would busily forget.
But like some sequel to the bird in Bede
which flies in one window and out the other,
this one paused, as if visited
by some avian rumination on the
condition of those who'd held him captive
and then returned him to the hopeful road.
In the air it paused a moment, like the dove
in Piero's *Trinity*, all spirit-hover

and silent verdict. Over the roofs it went —
toward the future, navigating by wingspan
its return to the place where life began
to commune with cloud and wind content.
It lived with me then, down the church-stopped slope,
and accompanies me now: why should it not
have flamed in colour, and vibrant hope?
It keeps in its feathers the symbol of spirit:
asking that we also, in our brief day, soar.
When we arrived at the doors and stopped
at the prayer-notice on the padlocked door,
we turned to find a sky of immortal birds.

ON THE TRISTAN CHORD

Finally it's clear: on this, everything depends.
If I listen with the right endeavour,
then the sea will accrue colour,
friends will learn to love one another
and animals I've not met at the other ends
of the world will prick up ears,
and remember how the world has rhymed.
The world is always curled and primed —
its instinct is to angle for us. Its impatience
is not that it aims to pass us by,
but that it longs to meet us before we die,
and persuade us of its own benevolence.
It wants the ache of irresolution cast off:
like a comic, it wants our attention, then our laugh.

VILLANELLE ON A HANDKERCHIEF TREE

And I was too late for this year's bloom:
when next year comes, we shall have moved:
life's a house with too many rooms.

The white spectacular petals have drifted home:
the handkerchief tree I've always loved
won't perform for me its Maytime bloom.

I don't think much of pessimism or gloom.
But disappointment can't always be shoved
aside — because life has such vacant rooms.

This is a world where grave and the womb
each have their truth — and each is proved:
I was late for the birth of this year's bloom.

What we missed out on, we can't exhume —
we can't expunge all the dirt we gloved.
Life's a house with such a lot of rooms.

To love the tree and ignore the tomb
still might be wisdom, and leave us unaggrieved.
I wish I'd been earlier to this year's bloom.
Life's a house of such unvisited rooms.

KITE

Suddenly, you burst out of a tangle of string,
the only one in Chiswick with a coherent
idea of what it meant to be free.

Your smiling mind went every which way:
into your future even, for you knew now
that if you could master wind and direction

anything was possible. And you raised the diamond
high, an emblem of that, and I could see your mind
delighting at the elements

which you now held in your small running hand.
And I've thought about it ever since,
picturing you rounding the corner as the kite flew,

as if you also knew what infinite joy
you were bestowing on those of us who were watching —
and especially on me,

who held you in my hand as this poem,
just as you held the kite in the region of your hand,
so suddenly older, so suddenly happier.

May that trajectory
of age giving way regularly to joy,
be the story the world has to tell of you.

OPERA REHEARSAL, HOLLAND PARK 2013

Summer will not sing more beautifully than this.
Verdi, I would guess, epiphanic and sudden,
grows out of the open-air rehearsal marquee
superimposing tone on neutrality:
the boy's football match finds its drama,
an elderly couple, their inveterate hands linked,
becomes first courtship, perhaps beside the Arno,
when a music like this went off in their minds.
The eventual concert, tense with the burden of money,
will intervene between listener and music
with the distractions of formality,
but now, the soprano gilds the pigeons with sun,
the drinks in the café are all ambrosial,
and we are taller, that much stronger, for this music.

THE PIANO

A piano is tuning up in Dolgellau.
Its ivories are pristine, newly dusted.
When the tuner nears a glazed eye
to hammer dust from strings, she finds them good.

I always assume there will be time
to enact those satisfactory days
every saint predicts, where roses climb
while a music to strike at sorrow plays.

A piano is tuning up in Dolgellau.
It will ignite what was always latent
in the heart's practice, remake the sky,
and tell what the hints of beauty meant.

I always assume a cautious confidence,
that a limit is placed somewhere on rage —
that in a place outside your experience,
a piano is tuned up to your advantage.

So I pack my suitcase for Dolgellau,
and make sure I flatten the sheet music:
nothing possesses such authority
as the brave attempts you're yet to make.

I never presume the road will be straight.
Gloucestershire will cede to the border;
and the sheep-thronged hills give us Gwynedd.
We'll go, knowing that if there's order

to be had, it must relate in time to this:
the keys on the other side of those slopes,
whose articulacy will taste of happiness
if their melody can be attuned to hope.

THE BUZZARD

The buzzard knows all history —
a kite whose chord is hunger
it hovers this realm of mouse and brake,
and dips with such talent earthwards
to the earthworm: leisure
always inhabits its amber eye.
The Mabinogion was written
and both Thomases had their day
under its aegis — wing-shadow
falling across the page in
shapes that drove the poets' hands.
The battles of Tintern and Ebrauc
had their outcomes and aftermaths
while it squawked, or closed claws
at the nape of the gentle rabbit.
While Dolgellau sent young wraiths
to dutiful deaths for a global cause,
or when a weird virus rushed to reveal
the hegemony of the very small,
still the buzzard soared and hovered,
in control of weather and event,
rushing down the sky only
to see what the rose-bush meant
when it rustled, or the lake
when it rippled. It held course,
and held court, in the wild cloud,
a thing which would endure
above and beyond our sake —
uninterested in progress,
pledged instead to truth.
In chasing down a vole's youth,

it chased down a buzzard's spirit.
From this low point, I adore it;
in my heart, I claim its wing:
the joy I've known has been
to feel a buzzard's breath
breathe along the stage,
and enter the song that I sing.

WISH LIST

I want my thieves to have a sense of humour;
my CEOs humility.
I want to behold arrogance in the poor
and trepidation in the free.

I want my monarch's nails black and dirty;
my vagabonds, immaculate;
the hero to be early for the ceremony
and the cap-in-hand, late.

The cantankerous must practise laughter;
the precocious slow down a bit;
the prime minister should enter after
the clamdigger. Clamdiggers are prophets.

I want to see the entirety of time
turned inside out like a crazy glove,
the free-versers discover rhyme;
the nihilist, the lunacy of love.

I want my fraudster to have a kindly smile;
and HMRC repent.
I want the tongue-tied to sing in gorgeous riddle,
and the comedians fall silent.

THE BAG

The dove, yours, was loose on the lawn —
and the whole garden-party watched
in horror as it crawled into my bag.

'Chris,' you said. 'My bird is in your bag.'

But how poorly packed it was:
cavernous as a soul,
a sports-bag roomier than you'd think.
Old clothes, squashed like a washing load,
dog-eared paperbacks, knotted phone-chargers,
chocolate wrappers, and an orange.
That day's bric-a-brac told how untidy
the untended life can get.

Occasionally, I sensed the dove twitching,
and rolled my sleeves,
plunging deeper into the bag:
a pair of shorts, a random bin-liner,
an apple core —
it was an increasingly embarrassing bag.

Soon the others grew bored of my search,
and went back to their patio conversation,
while I fiddled endlessly,
looking for a flit of feather,
or the stored strength of a wing.

THE BLADE

I raise the blade.
Its cupboard-shadow —
like the idea of itself —
follows me across the room,
a sleek suggestion stalking me.
Outside, is one of December's ebbings-away,
and light withdrawn towards Normandy.
Inside, I follow the blade.

The kitchen-light is tactile at its edge,
showing the infinities of the room —
angles, receedings, dimensions.
I hold the skies under which the blade was needed,
I turn the trees we learned to slay with blades
and twist again my half-nervous hold
until light grows off its surface,
like the inspiration behind its invention,
routing its own shadow
like some restaged arrival of the blade.

Tonight the blade will sleep
in the knife-holder sheathed,
its utility stored in modern shapes of wood.
It's prehistory, hiding among amenity:
the first sharpening on savannas,
the vitality of the blade thought-of and perfected —
calling up the slicings and dicings,
another cooking, a subtler food.
This Christmas night
when the sky is a vineyard graped with stars,
and the family are padding back from carols,

I turn away from them
and privately,
with a prayer-like thought which is no prayer,
honour the blade.

AFTER IBSEN: THE REINDEER

That's me, there on the highest crag,
crawling trenches-style, on tensed elbows.
Gully to the left of me, where it's known
oblivion, one mistake away, must lie —
an aspect of the sheerness of the sky.
Here to my right reigns the sparse earth,
where the invention of life almost sags;
the tulips protest the dry dead grasses;
and life is reduced to the looseness of scree.
But I've seen a creature grazing here,
where so few hunters come. I know my worth.
I'll hunt it. And the verdict of renown
after I return from these upper passes
will be the antlers I'll wear as a crown.

There. Raised so you can hardly see it,
and coming out of mist: mute and high up
where the climber can't know the scale of the drop.
Not even a reindeer, but a reindeer's shape —
delicate as a blown bubble about to pop.
Now I stand, and trapeze the fine line.
Rubble tumbles, dislodged by my feet.
In balance, intent on my enterprise,
I continue, fearless about ending-up —
until I pounce — now! — at the creature's nape,
my fingers skilled pincers: hooked twine.
The stubborn creature wrestles my attack —
bucking, and rucking, a sudden-tough prize.
I summon the strength to fight back.

Now I have that prince of beasts in a lock —
but the scrabbly dirt has soon to give,
and even my footing must betray me: I rave
at the air — at lengths of descending grave —
and flail down levels, keeping my hold alive,
tense for the hard smack. Rather than death
comes reflection's mockery in the loch:
an exact rushing-up. It will unify
endeavour and falling-short in water's weave.
Then we're at a grapple, fighting for breath:
this is something we'll do as a pair,
my powers in league with compliant reality:
like this, I seize and ensnare the reindeer.

THE DREAM SCULPTOR

I woke as a sculptor, authoring worlds in my hands:
That first time, raddled with sleep, I fumbled badly —
my materials twisted along the waking air.
Their flight was too nimble; I fell back, exhausted.

I hardly knew the motives behind composition;
I didn't understand my obligation to begin.
But now is momentum; now is need of those shapes.
I no longer pause in doubt: when I awaken,

a hand is frog-tongue-quick, and the opening
of any day is efficient recall,
and instant building with what I clutch, the leftover dream.

No sooner has the morning burst like juice from an orange,
crowned in light at the outer sky,
than I've a sculpture pocketed in advance of the day.

THE LION REVISITED

And so I contest the cities of this world:
coached in alertness, but caught in ineptitude,
never seeing what is hunting me.
I know it wants to kill me. Increasingly,
I've come to accept its ultimate victory:
I'll be happiest once it's eating my heart.

MARCH, 2020

Life is beginning to quiver in the leaf
and Christ is returning to the buds.
There is sway of potential, even in grief.
Change sweeps through on the unjust and the just.

When I next skirt this hemlock and cow parsley,
it shall be like the aftermath of the floods.
None shall populate the solar ambit of day:
change shall sweep through on the unjust and the just.

I shall be on death's other side, stricken
amid the glory-light of ceanothus,
watching the nurses and the scooter-children:
change shall sweep through on the unjust and the just.

I do not know if I am good or an outrage;
but shall hope the best of us is held in trust,
and that the world shall have a moral and an adage:
change shall sweep through on the unjust and the just.

CAEDMON

I had a dream, a dream to drain all doubt;
praise the peaceable, and promise yourself
reverence that the resurrection was written.
I shall ascend heavenly heights, and hope for
saints and seraphs, and strings amid the stars.
What is wide and wonderful will be with
and in meaning: mightily it has been made.
God did this: grew the abyss then grassed it,
favoured fractal, fulfilled phenomena.
Splendours sang out on the sand and in the cities.
Humankind was His chief happiness:
He stippled the star-roof and spheres for sinners,
made majesty that it might be made, marred,
and recreated in Christ the Pantocrator.

THE CLOAK

Life must make good
all our sufferings —
make pain a brother,
turn murder to dancing,
and knit out of dread
a cloak which cannot rend —
one so radiant and fine,
and piercingly divine,
it can be seen from one end
of the universe to the other.

ACKNOWLEDGEMENTS

Thanks are due to the editors of the following publications where versions of these poems previously appeared: 14, *Acumen, Ambit,* BBC *Radio 4, Eureka Street, Finito World, Ink, Sweat and Tears, The Journal, Littoral, Lockdown and After, London Grip, Mace, The Poet's Quest for God, Poetry Salzburg Review, Revival, Sunfish.* I especially want to thank Todd Swift for his wonderful edit of these poems during his recovery from illness.